Charlie Brown

and Snoopy

Selected cartoons from
As You Like It, Charlie Brown Vol. I

by CHARLES M. SCHULZ

A FAWCETT CREST BOOK

Fawcett Publications, Inc., Greenwich, Conn.

CHARLIE BROWN AND SNOOPY

This book, prepared especially for Fawcett Publications, Inc.,
comprises the first half of *AS YOU LIKE IT, CHARLIE BROWN,*
and is reprinted by arrangement with Holt, Rinehart & Winston, Inc.

Copyright © 1963, 1964 by United Feature Syndicate, Inc.

Printed in the United States of America
November 1970

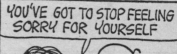

YOU WON'T DO IT, HUH?

NOPE!

I WANT PEOPLE TO HAVE MORE TO SAY ABOUT ME AFTER I'M GONE THAN, "HE WAS A NICE GUY... HE CHASED STICKS!"

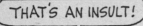

NINETY-FIVE, NINETY-SIX, NINETY-SEVEN..

NINETY-EIGHT, NINETY-NINE, ONE HUNDRED! HERE I COME...READY OR NOT!

WHAT ARE YOU STANDING HERE FOR? YOU'RE SUPPOSED TO BE HIDING!

I LIKE TO LISTEN TO YOU COUNT..

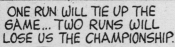

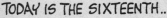

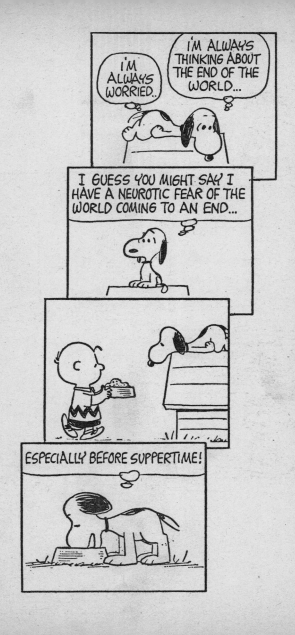

SO YOU'RE NOT GOING TO SCHOOL MONDAY, HUH, SALLY?

OH, YES, I'M GOING... I CHANGED MY MIND...

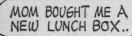

MOM BOUGHT ME A NEW LUNCH BOX..

I FIGURED IF MOM WENT TO ALL THE TROUBLE AND EXPENSE OF GETTING ME A NEW LUNCH BOX, I'D BETTER GO TO SCHOOL...

BUT THAT'S THE ONLY REASON I'M GOING!

STUPID DOG!

THAT'S HIS "HA HA..YOU HAVE TO GO TO SCHOOL, AND I DON'T" DANCE!

SNOOPY'S IN THE HOSPITAL?

UH HUH...DIDN'T YOU KNOW? HE'S BEEN THERE FOR ABOUT FOUR DAYS...

IS HE ALLOWED TO HAVE VISITORS?

OH, YES...HE'S HAD A FEW CLOSE FRIENDS DROP BY ALREADY...

DEAR SNOOPY,
I MISS YOU MORE
THAN I CAN SAY.

I HOPE THEY ARE
TREATING YOU WELL
IN THE HOSPITAL.

WHILE YOU ARE THERE, WHY
DON'T YOU HAVE THEM GIVE
YOU A FLEA BATH?

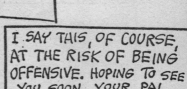

I SAY THIS, OF COURSE,
AT THE RISK OF BEING
OFFENSIVE. HOPING TO SEE
YOU SOON. YOUR PAL,
CHARLIE BROWN

WHAT'S THIS ABOUT NOT BEING ABLE TO LOOK AT THE ECLIPSE?

IT'S VERY DANGEROUS... YOU COULD SUFFER SEVERE BURNS OF THE RETINA FROM INFRA-RED RAYS

BUT WHAT'S THE SENSE IN HAVING AN ECLIPSE IF YOU CAN'T **LOOK** AT IT?

SOMEBODY IN PRODUCTION SURE SLIPPED UP THIS TIME!

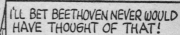

OUR FAMILY NAME IS 95472.. ACTUALLY THAT'S OUR ZIP CODE NUMBER...

IN FACT, THAT WAS THE NUMBER THAT SORT OF STARTED THE WHOLE THING...THAT WAS THE NUMBER THAT FINALLY CAUSED MY DAD TO BECOME COMPLETELY HYSTERICAL ONE NIGHT

MY FULL NAME IS 555 95472, BUT EVERYONE CALLS ME 5 FOR SHORT...I HAVE TWO SISTERS NAMED 3 AND 4

THOSE ARE NICE FEMININE NAMES...

WE THINK SO

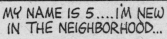

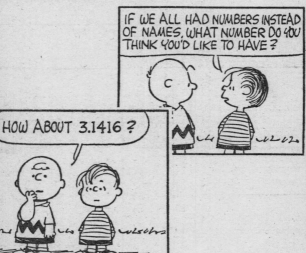

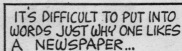

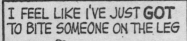

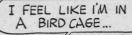

ONCE THERE WAS A TIME WHEN I THOUGHT I COULD GIVE UP THUMB-SUCKING...

NOW I DOUBT IF I EVER COULD..

I'M HOOKED!

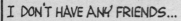

HE KNOWS WHICH KIDS HAVE BEEN GOOD AND WHICH KIDS HAVE BEEN BAD...

AND ON HALLOWEEN NIGHT THE "GREAT PUMPKIN" RISES OUT OF THE PUMPKIN PATCH, AND FLIES THROUGH THE AIR WITH HIS BAG OF TOYS FOR ALL THE GOOD CHILDREN IN THE WORLD!

HOW LONG HAS IT BEEN SINCE YOU'VE HAD A PHYSICAL CHECK-UP?

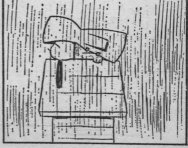

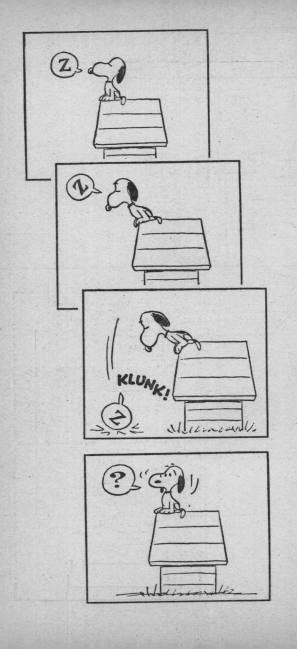

NOW Peanuts Jewelry

Each item is 14 Kt. gold finish, hand-crafted cloisonné in brilliant colors, exquisitely designed by Aviva. Items shown in actual size. Complete satisfaction guaranteed or money refunded.

No. 10 pin $3

No. 11 pin $3

No. 12 pin $3

No. 13A pierced $3
No. 13B non-pierced $3

No. 14 pin $3

No. 15 pin $3

No. 16 pin $3

No. 17A pierced $3
No. 17B non-pierced $3

No. 18 pin $3

No. 19 pin $3

No. 20 pin $3

No. 21 pin $3

More Peanuts Jewelry
See Previous Page

No. 22 tie tack $3

No. 23 tie tack $3

No. 24 key chain $3

No. 25 money clip $4

No. 26 tie tack $3

No. 27 tie bar $3

No. 28 cufflinks $4

No. 29 pin $3

Please specify identity number of each item ordered and add 25¢ for each item to cover postage and handling. Personal check or money order. No cash. Send orders to HAMILTON HOUSE, Cos Cob, Conn. 06807.